Lions

Leo Statts

abdopublishing.com

Published by Abdo Zoom™, PO Box 398166, Minneapolis, Minnesota 55439. Copyright © 2017 by Abdo Consulting Group, Inc. International copyrights reserved in all countries. No part of this book may be reproduced in any form without written permission from the publisher. Abdo Zoom™ is a trademark and logo of Abdo Consulting Group, Inc.

Printed in the United States of America, North Mankato, Minnesota
062016
092016

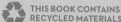

Cover Photo: Photocreo Michal Bednarek/Shutterstock Images
Interior Photos: Eric Isselee/Shutterstock Images, 1; Rob Hainer/Shutterstock Images, 4; iStockphoto, 5, 6, 9, 14, 15 (top), 15 (bottom); W. L. Davies/iStockphoto, 7, 8, 18; Shutterstock Images, 10–11, 13; Red Line Editorial, 11, 20 (left), 20 (right), 21 (left), 21 (right); Jason Prince/Shutterstock Images, 12; Jez Bennett/iStockphoto, 16–17; Maggy Meyer/iStockphoto, 19

Editor: Emily Temple
Series Designer: Madeline Berger
Art Direction: Dorothy Toth

Publisher's Cataloging-in-Publication Data
Names: Statts, Leo, author.
Title: Lions / by Leo Statts.
Description: Minneapolis, MN : Abdo Zoom, [2017] | Series: Savanna animals | Includes bibliographical references and index.
Identifiers: LCCN 2016941161 | ISBN 9781680792027 (lib. bdg.) | ISBN 9781680793703 (ebook) | ISBN 9781680794595 (Read-to-me ebook)
Subjects: LCSH: Lions--Juvenile literature.
Classification: DDC 599.757--dc23
LC record available at http://lccn.loc.gov/2016941161

Table of Contents

Lions 4

Body 8

Habitat 10

Food 14

Life Cycle 18

Quick Stats. 20

Glossary 22

Booklinks 23

Index 24

Lions

Lions are big cats.
They are fierce.

They are called
"King of the Jungle."

Their roars
are loud.

They can be heard miles away!

Body

Male lions can weigh 440 pounds (200 kg).

Lions have gold
or brown fur.
An adult male
has a **mane**.

Habitat

Lions live in Africa and India. You can find them in grassy **plains**. They also live in open **savannas**.

Where lions live

Most lions live in groups.
The groups are called **prides**.

Each pride has its own **territory**.

Food

Lions eat meat.

They eat
antelope.

They also
eat zebras.

Female lions do
most of the hunting.

They usually hunt in groups.

Lions have one to six babies.
Baby lions are called cubs.

Lions live 10 to 15 years in the wild.

Average Length

A lion is about
as long as a sofa.

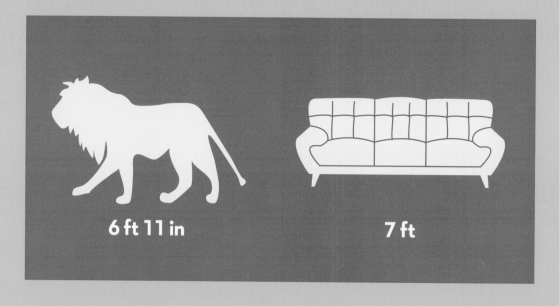

6 ft 11 in   7 ft

Average Weight

A male lion weighs less than a baby grand piano.

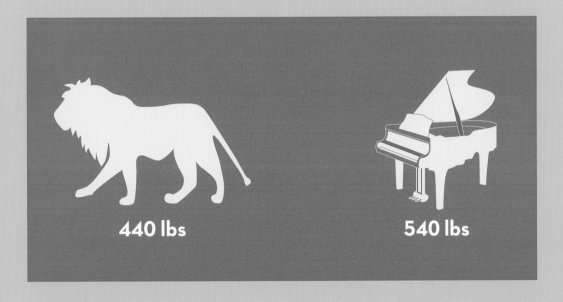

440 lbs

540 lbs

Glossary

cub - a young animal.

mane - the longer hair that grows on an animal's neck and back.

plain - an area of dry, grassy land.

pride - a group of lions living together.

savanna - a grassland with few or no trees.

territory - an area that animals live in and guard.

Booklinks

For more information
on lions, please visit
booklinks.abdopublishing.com

Zoom In on Animals!

Learn even more with the Abdo Zoom
Animals database. Check out
abdozoom.com for more information.

Index

baby, 18

cats, 4

eat, 14, 15

fur, 9

groups, 12, 17

hunting, 16

live, 10, 11, 12, 19

mane, 9

roars, 6

weigh, 8